WIT AND WISDOM

OF GOOD POPE JOHN

WIT

AND WISDOM

OF

GOOD POPE JOHN

Collected by HENRI FESQUET

Translated by Salvator Attanasio

✦✳✦✿✦✳✦✿✦✳

P. J. Kenedy & Sons · New York

PUBLISHER'S NOTE

The publishers are indebted to Mr. Norman Cousins for permission to use as a Foreword to this book his editorial on Pope John XXIII which appeared in the *Saturday Review*, issue of June 15, 1963.

This book was originally published in France under the title *Les Fioretti du Bon Pape Jean* © Librairie Arthème Fayard, 1963.

LC Catalog Card Number 64–21846
Manufactured in the United States of America
Design by Stefan Salter

✢※✣✤✢※✣✤✢※

CONTENTS

Foreword by NORMAN COUSINS   7

Preface to the French Edition
    by Pastor MARC BOEGNER   13

Preamble. An Easygoing Man   19

  1. I Am Only the Pope   31

  2. First Gestures   37

  3. Characteristics   47

  4. Humor   67

  5. Variations   75

  6. Favorite Maxims   83

· 5

Contents

7. The Daughters of Eve   87

8. The Temple of Creation   93

9. Blessed Are the Poor   101

10. The Self-Styled Great of This World   107

11. The World's Twaddle   111

12. War: A Contradiction   117

13. Communists   121

14. Love Your Enemies   127

15. The Prophets of Doom   133

16. Let the Little Children Come to Me   137

17. Sacred Freedom   143

18. Good and Bad Theology   149

19. A Council? Fresh Air   153

20. The Church? A Public Fountain   159

21. Count the Sheep One by One   163

22. That They May Be One   169

23. The Two Wings of Truth and Goodness   175

24. Our Sister, Death   181

Epilogue. The House of All   189

FOREWORD

NORMAN COUSINS, Editor, *Saturday Review*

He leaned forward in his chair and smiled. "When I meet a person and talk to him privately, I try to put him at ease by reminding him that I am the same as he is: I have two eyes, a nose—a very large nose—mouth, two ears, and so forth. Even so, people sometimes remain rigid and incommunicative. You must feel completely relaxed. We will talk as man to man." And again he smiled.

I handed him a letter expressing the President's concern and good wishes for his health.

"I get many messages these days from people who pray that my illness is without great pain. Pain is no foe of mine. I have memories. Wonderful memories. I have lived a long life and I have much to look back upon. These memories give me great joy now and fill my life. There is really no room for the pain.

"There is so much to think back upon. When I was young, I was an Apostolic delegate in Bulgaria. I came to know and admire the Slavic peoples. I tried to study the Slavic languages, including the Russian. I never became really proficient but I did learn to read the language to some extent. I am sorry I never pursued these studies. Do you know the Russian language?"

"No."

"A pity. You really ought to learn it. You are much younger than I. It wouldn't take you very long. A very important language. The Russian people, a very wonderful people. We must not condemn them because we do not like their political system. They have a deep spiritual heritage. This they have not lost. We can talk to them. Right now, we have to talk to them. We must always try to speak to the good in people. Nothing can be lost by trying. Everything can be lost if men do not find some way to work together to save the peace. I am not afraid to talk to anyone about peace on earth. If Mr. Khrushchev were sitting right where you are sitting now, I don't think I would feel uneasy or awkward in talking to him. We both come from small villages. We both have peasant backgrounds. We would understand one another."

Again he smiled.

"Much depends now on keeping open and strengthening all possible lines of communications. During the terrible crisis over Cuba in October, the possibility of a nuclear holocaust became very real. I asked the statesmen to exercise the greatest restraint and to do all that had to be done to reduce the terrible tension. My appeal was given prominent attention inside the Soviet Union. I was glad that this was so. This is a good sign."

His voice betrayed his fatigue and general sense of depletion, but he spoke with eagerness. There wasn't too much time left to him personally (our discussion took place in December 1962), but he was determined to use himself fully as long as he could in the service of world peace. The Holy See might be useful in reducing tensions between East and West. Therefore it was logical to open up contacts. The Holy See was not attempting to arrogate to itself an unwelcome or unnatural role. But the grimly significant feature of the present world crisis was precisely that there were so many elements of danger and so few elements of control. Any person or agency in a position, near or far, to help strengthen the controls had a positive obligation to do so.

Did he know that his efforts were likely to be criticized or misconstrued? Certainly, but this was no warrant for lack of initiative or irresponsible inaction. The worst that could be said was that the Pope was taking Christianity literally. He couldn't imagine Jesus concurring in the notion that human security and freedom depended on the manufacture and amassing of hydrogen bombs which, if used, would put a torch to the human nest. The fact that two or more nations, in the act of warring against one another, would in actuality also be at war with the human race—if this fact had no profound moral and spiritual significance, then what fact did?

This question, along with all the other central questions related to peace and the human future, formed the basis of the historic encyclical, *Peace on Earth,* in April. A few weeks later, the progressive nature of his illness became critical. Even so, he followed events carefully. He looked for evidence that the nations were making progress in organizing their relationships and halting the arms race. He was heartened by the worldwide response to his plea for peace. His hopes were never higher than at the end. Some men will recognize that a claim has thus been laid on them in terms of their own efforts and obligations. The sustaining prospect is that there may be enough of them.

We live in an age which looks to physical motion for its spectacular achievements. A man encased in a metallic capsule spinning through outer space; the heart of an atom pried open and releasing vast stores of energy; streams of electrons flashing images of something happening thousands of miles away—these are the main articles of wonder in the modern world. But they do not have the impress on history of an eighty-one-year-old man dying of cancer, using the Papacy to make not just his own church but all churches fully relevant and fully alive in the cause of human unity and peace.

Human advocacy harnessed to powerful ideas continues to be the prime power. The peace sought by Pope John need not be unattainable once belief in ideas is put ahead of belief in moving parts.

※✦✶❀✦✶❀✦❀

PREFACE TO THE FRENCH EDITION

Pastor MARC BOEGNER of the French Academy

Several hours after the death of Pope John XXIII,
Pastor Westphal, President of the Federation of French
Protestants, was asked how French Protestants felt
about the deceased Pontiff. Pastor Westphal replied:
"No doubt it is the first time that we Protestants are in
mourning for a pope." Indeed, it is very true that many
of us have grieved over the departure from this world
of the humble and courageous Pontiff whom God has
summoned to His presence.

Why this deep feeling of loss and sorrow? Was it because John XXIII, after having taken the initiative in
convoking a Council that is of concern to all Churches

and to all Christians, would not be able to lead it to the consummation of its great purpose? After the first session of the Council had aroused such high hopes in us we were painfully affected by a death which opened the way to grave uncertainties. Yet he whom we mourned was not the Pope but the disciple of Jesus Christ, one whose heart was inflamed by love, who radiated the spirit of poverty sung in the Beatitudes, who offered his life for the renewal of his Church, for Christian unity and for peace in the world.

As we read the *Fioretti* that Henri Fesquet has gathered in this volume, we reverentially and gratefully discover in its moving transparency a soul suffused in light, a heart of infinite tenderness, a mind full of good sense. We discover, in short, a man who had been a priest, bishop and pope but who always remained deeply human, very close to his fellow men, especially to the poor and the little people, ever ready to love and to serve them.

Obviously all the utterances collected here are not of the same spiritual depth. But taken as a whole, in which so much humor is joined with so much goodness, so much humility with supernatural greatness, they instill an authentic Christian joy in those who listen to them in the same simplicity of spirit with which they were delivered.

As I read them, I was reminded of another son of the Roman Church who one day was to disclose hidden and unsuspected capacities: the Abbé Couturier. He was the man of God to whom we owe in great part the magnificent fruits being yielded with ever growing abundance by the octaves of prayer for Christian unity. Of John XXIII also it can be said that when he became the successor of Pius XII nobody suspected the unique vocation to which he was to respond so quickly. What splendors are suddenly revealed in the action of grace which chooses whom it wills in order that the designs of the living God's love may be accomplished!

Let us be grateful to Henri Fesquet for acquainting us with these good sayings of Pope John, so filled with the pure vitality of the Gospel. This is also an excellent opportunity for me to express my appreciation of his clear, knowledgeable and frequently stirring articles on the Council in *Le Monde*. Thanks to them, we were drawn into the very midst of the deliberations of the Council and experienced the joy of confirming that this impressive assembly and the one who confers his authority upon it remain faithful to the intentions and to the spirit of John XXIII. This knowledge strengthens the hopes of all Christians who look forward to the restoration of Christian unity on the day that it will please God to make it a reality.

"*Naturalness is found in simplicity, and divinity in naturalness.*"

"*Ever since I entered the priesthood, I have placed myself at the disposal of Holy Church. I have served her without anxiety, without ambition. That's all there is, nothing else. It is unnecessary to look further.*"

JOHN XXIII

PREAMBLE

AN EASYGOING MAN

✣✤✥✦✧✦✥✤✣

　＋✦＋＋✦＋*

What is a pope?

We were perhaps on the point of forgetting, when John XXIII came on the scene to refresh our memories. Certainly, this does not mean to say that his predecessor, Pius XII, was not a great pope; the lofty and many qualities of that exceptional man had attracted the attention of the whole world. But, as Georges Hubert wrote in *La Croix:* "If Pius XI inspired respect and Pius XII admiration, John XXIII aroused affection, indeed more: love."

We were on the point of forgetting what a pope is: a pope is not only the vicar of Jesus Christ, a man of prayer, a maker of pronouncements, an ascetic, a doctor, a scholar, a sovereign pontiff, a head of State, a man of the world, a stained-glass figure, a profile on a medallion. A pope is also, to put it simply, a man, the first among the bishops, a pastor, the father beloved by unbelievers, the brother of the humble of the earth, a person in whom one wants to confide in the certainty of being understood. He is the representative of the Jesus of Bethlehem, of Bethany, of the Sermon on the Mount and of the discourse at the Last Supper. It would not be seemly to compare John XXIII with Pius XII, but it is a fact that Pope John's popularity had no common measure with that of his predecessors.

Why was this? Because these qualities were immediately perceptible and perceived in the person of the good Pontiff, people were immediately struck by them. Our democratic age, so demanding with regard to the "great" and so responsive to simplicity and to spontaneity, saw in the person of Pope John the pope of whom it was in such dire need and for whom it no longer dared to hope.

Yes, Pope John surpassed all expectations. Not only because he was not the transitional pope on whom his electors had reckoned, but because nobody, not even the most perspicacious, could have foreseen the revolution he was to bring about in the customs of the Papacy, his aptitude for making himself accessible to those farthest removed, his tropism toward the values of the modern world, his opening not so much "to the left," as it has been called without due consideration, but to all the aspirations of an era stirred by a passion for justice, tolerance and brotherhood. A Sardinian miner expressed this for us in his picturesque vocabulary: "John XXIII was neither white, nor black, nor red. He had no color. He was everybody's man, the Pope of peace: that is why everyone listened to him and loved him."

Who in superficial Paris was able to divine such a powerful personality behind the Nuncio's good nature? Just before the opening of the conclave which elected him, a French archbishop was asked: "Who in your opinion will be elected pope?" Disdainfully the prelate replied: "Some kind of a Roncalli." Msgr. Chappoulie, bishop of Angers, a man of the upper classes, literally wept with grief on learning of the choice that had been made by the Sacred College.

The secret of his success is the mystery of a soul, the mystery of grace itself. Let us therefore respect it. It can never be sufficiently stressed that John XXIII made a breach in the wall which cuts off the Church from the world of the humble and the hungry. Death overtook him before he could institute spectacular reforms in this domain.[1] Nevertheless the Council which

---

[1] When Pastor Roger Schütz, prior of the community of Taizé, expressed the hope that the Vatican might become less ornate and more evangelical in its external aspects, the gist of the Pope's reply was: "Patience, patience! I can't do everything at once."

he managed to impose on a reluctant Curia, jealous of its prerogatives, engendered a state of mind and set an irreversible impulse in motion. Sooner or later, the Church will again find the countenance of poverty which the Bride of Christ should never have lost.

As will be seen in these pages, John XXIII multiplied his deeds and words in order to show his love for the poor and for Lady Poverty. He put himself on an equal footing with the people by his disdain for honors, by his aversion to luxury, by his exquisite cordiality. He "de-mythicized" the profession of pope. John XXIII is the only pope of modern times about whom a Communist worker could say: "There's a man I'd gladly sit down to have a drink with!" In his presence one did not feel himself being judged, but loved for what one was.

Was Pope John a demagogue? Some parlor imbeciles still drop this slanderous tidbit between cocktails. Yet no one was less a demagogue than this Pope who always maintained his dignity in his very spontaneity. He was a stranger to flattery and his courtesy sprang from the heart.

The Pope was neither an intellectual nor a theoretician. He loved history, "the teacher of life." This intuitive son of peasant parents had an acute sense of timing. He knew how to wait, how to let situations ripen and minds evolve according to their own pace. *"Gutta cavat lapidem"* (Drops of water hollow out a stone) was one of his maxims. He had scant appreciation for theologians. "They are the ones who got us into our present-day difficulties," said the Pope one day to a non-Catholic observer at the Council. "It's up to ordinary Christians like you and me to extricate ourselves from them." In fact, a theologian too often—happily, not always—is a system-builder and loses the sense of life. Pope John's anti-intellectualism inevitably recalls that of Francis of Assisi. Should we not glimpse something of a revelatory character in the future Pope's amusing outburst regarding Teilhard de Chardin whom he was later to defend against the convict-wardens of orthodoxy: "You people in France are always raising problems. Why do you need to discuss man's origins? Teach your faithful the *Pater,* the *Ave,* the *Credo,* the fourteen works of mercy and *basta!*"

Pope John XXIII, this corpulent man who enjoyed life, this lover of good food,[2] broad of features and heavy of gait was—oh miracle!—an easygoing man, extraordinarily nimble in spirit. He possessed in the highest degree a quality truly exceptional in a pope—a sense of humor, that virtue which Oscar Cullmann, in a lecture he gave at the Sorbonne, called a *specifically Christian* virtue.

The stodgy-minded still can't get over it! A pope who cracked jokes, who winked his eye, who let fly witticisms, who improvised even in the most delicate

[2] Pope John occasionally had brought in from France the Roquefort and Burgundy from which, along with some bread, he made his usual evening meal.

situations.[3] No longer can one say: "As serious as a pope!" John XXIII never pontificated.

A nonconformist, he would decide on the spur of the moment to present a gift to a visitor (as when he gave his own breviary to an Anglican canon), to go out for a walk, to visit a sick friend. For example, panic seized his entourage when on the eve of the Council he decided to go on a pilgrimage to Loretto and Assisi.

Indeed, this old man had a mind and a heart as alert and agile as those of an adolescent. By nature he was as smiling and serene as others are anxious and tense. "Thank God," he said one day, "I have no trouble with my liver." Far from complicating simple matters, he had the art of simplifying complicated ones. He was a man of great good sense and fine judgment. It was no doubt for these qualities that Pius XII appointed him nuncio to Paris during the tragic and tension-ridden time following France's Liberation.

Pope John's total abandonment to the divine will assumed heroic dimensions. During the interminable agony of his last days, while the whole world watched with bated breath, everyone, including the most indifferent, understood that all his amiability concealed a soul suffused with grace and a sanctity of the most authentic character. Cardinal Léger, the archbishop of Montreal, expressed to us his amazement that a world,

[3] It happened that on several occasions the *Osservatore Romano* did not dare to print this or that remark of the Pope, or else went to great pains to minimize its meaning.

apparently so materialistic and in such horror of death, could have kept its eyes and its heart fixed for days and nights on this dying man and suffer with him.

The death of good Pope John was truly the apotheosis of his life. If we were in the Middle Ages, John XXIII would have been canonized by the people. *Vox populi, vox Dei!*

The following pages are before all else a gesture of filial devotion. Immense indeed is our gratitude to a pope who was able to restore confidence in the Roman Church to so many men of good will, disappointed and disconcerted by ecclesiastical trappings, arrogance, narrowness of spirit and pettiness. Too many clerics are still disdainful of the virtues of today's world. Do they not accord more importance to protocol and the subtleties of diplomacy than to the audacities of charity, to temporal means rather than to spiritual power, to the letter of regulations rather than to the sap of the Gospel? In less time than it took for us to become aware of it, John XXIII knew how to reconcile the Church with our era.

Thanks to this Pope, the man in the street, on whom bourgeois Catholics bestow little love or interest, has grasped something of the mystery of the Church and of the Gospel. The Church has once more become the Church of all, even of unbelievers. John XXIII replaced anathemas by mercy. He opened doors and windows. He stretched out his arms to the whole world. He obliterated distances and circled around obstacles with a gesture, with a word, with a smile.

John XXIII prepared the way for Paul VI, apostle of the Gentiles. The Church—at last—no longer fears the high seas. In the innermost reaches of his soul Pope John replied to the pressing question of Christ: "Peter, do you love me more than the others?" And all else was erased before this greater love.

Others have written biographies of John XXIII. Ours is a more modest aim: to let the Pope draw his own portrait, as it were, by way of sayings, anecdotes, or recollections of serious or amusing occasions. This will allow ordinary folk, who have neither the inclination nor the time to pour over learned volumes, to grasp something of the interior energies and impulses of a real "pastor" who had the whole world as his parish and governed it with an evangelical simplicity.

The resemblance between Pope John and St. Francis of Assisi, lover of poverty, singer of nature, poet and mystic, is striking. We hope that by leafing through these *Fioretti* the reader will experience the same joy that we had in arranging them. There is a kind of spiritual comfort to be found in the company of John XXIII. We feel a desire to linger as with a friend and, at least for a few minutes, we become better persons.

I arranged this garland of recollections in a tiny Sardinian village between the sky and the sea—a first cousin to Sotto il Monte—assisted by my wife and my young children. I take this occasion to thank all those who have given me permission to reproduce the anecdotes which they related to us in confidence, and even those who, for modesty's sake no doubt, did not allow themselves to be questioned. Their discretion will make it possible, perhaps, to publish a more substantial collection after certain hypersensitivities shall have been erased by time. This will be to the greater glory, not of beloved Pope John but of Him whose humble servant was all that he wished to be.

HENRI FESQUET

1
I AM ONLY THE POPE

✛※⤫✛✛⊕✛✛※✛⤫⊕✛✛※

A MAN LIKE EVERY OTHER MAN

"You have been awaiting me anxiously, and things have been written and said about me which go beyond my merits. Humbly I now present myself. I am like every other man who lives here below. I am seventy-one years of age. I have been endowed with the grace of good physical health, with a little good sense that enables me to look quickly and clearly into the heart of things, and with a disposition to love mankind which keeps me faithful to the injunctions of the Gospel, respectful of my rights and those of others, and which prevents me doing harm to anyone."

(Address upon his arrival in Venice.)

As Patriarch of Venice, Cardinal Roncalli expressed the desire to serve the Mass of one of his nephews, a young priest.

When the latter protested, the Patriarch replied: "I'm sorry, but I absolutely insist upon it. I want to see if you know how to celebrate the Mass properly."

✢✻✲☯✢✻✲☯✢✻

One day while Nuncio in Paris, Msgr. Roncalli paid a visit to one of his cousins, a wine-grower in southern France. His kinsman not only bore the family name Roncalli but also had the same first name as the Nuncio, Angelo. At the end of the dinner, which was held in the common room of the farmhouse, the future Pope helped his relative to bring the animals back to the stable.

✢✻✲☯✢✻✲☯✢✻

"The representative of the highest spiritual authority of the earth is glad, indeed boasts, of being the son of a humble but robust and honest laborer."

(To the Mayor of Fleury-sur-Loire.)

✢✻✲☯✢✻✲☯✢✻

On the day following his election, John XXIII summoned Count dalla Torre, editorial director of the *Osservatore Romano,* to a private audience. The editor had not been so honored in twelve years. The Pope expressed his interest in questions concerning the press and promised the Count his support. But he insisted that henceforth the *Osservatore Romano* avoid using the customary superlative formulas such as "august lips," "illumined by grace," etc.

"Simply write 'the Pope said so and so, the Pope did so and so . . .'" he instructed the Count.

Truth obliges us to say that he was hardly obeyed on this point.

AFTER ALL . . .

When someone asked John XXIII for a favor which he feared he would be unable to grant, he would say, as if to excuse himself: "After all, I'm only the Pope!"

⤳✳⤳✿⤳✳⤳✿⤳✳

One day John XXIII decided to stop in at a nursing-home run by nuns in order to visit a prelate who lay at death's door. He rang the bell. The Sister on duty thought she would faint from emotion when she saw the Pope standing in front of her.

"No need to be alarmed, Sister," he said. "After all, I'm only the Pope. Go get your superior."

And Pope John cooled his heels like anybody else until the superior arrived.

THE LAST PLACE

"The sense of my smallness and of my nothingness has always been my good companion, keeping me humble and content and granting me the joy of consecrating myself as best I can to the uninterrupted exercise of obedience and charity."

"I come from humble beginnings, and I was raised in a restraining, blessed poverty whose needs are few and which assures the growth of the highest and noblest virtues, and prepares one for the great ascents of life."

✢✳✧✲✢✳✧✲✢✳

"In my life I have always sought for the last place."

✢✳✧✲✢✳✧✲✢✳

"To accept the honor and the burden of the pontificate with simplicity, with the joy of being able to say that we have done nothing to bring it about, really nothing. Even more, to accept it with the formal and conscientious concern to avoid any gesture that might draw attention to one's person."

"I am the servant of servants."

(At St. Peter's Basilica.)

2
FIRST GESTURES

‍‍‍‍‍‍‍‍‍‍✤✻✛❂✤✻✛❂✤✻

THE POPE'S FIRST MEAL

At the end of the conclave, when Cardinal Tisserant stepped forward to announce to Cardinal Roncalli the choice of the cardinals, the newly elected Pope replied in Latin:

"Hearing your voice, I am made to tremble and I fear. What I know of my poverty and my littleness suffices for my confusion. But seeing in the votes of my brothers, the most excellent Cardinals of our Holy Roman Church, the sign of God's will, I accept the election they have made, and I lower my head and bend my back before the chalice of bitterness and to the yoke of the Cross. In the solemnity of Christ the King, we have all sung: 'The Lord is our Judge, the Lord is our Lawgiver, the Lord is our King: He will save us.'"

Then suddenly, as if to break the thread of his thoughts, John XXIII, according to one cardinal, is supposed to have added: "Now it's time to eat. Let's go to the table!"

But the following night was spent by the Pope in prayer.

✧✻✦☺✧✻✦☺✧✻

"What did I feel upon learning that I had been elected Pope? Much emotion, to be sure, and a host of anxieties. But also the same sensation as a baby in swaddling clothes, because the cassock which they had slipped over me was very tight and I felt as though I were wrapped up like a mummy."

UNPACKING HIS BELONGINGS

On taking possession of his apartments, the Pope sat on a packing case reading his breviary while the movers were putting his furniture in place. After finishing his reading, he left to explore the rooms which were still unfamiliar to him. When he came to a salon where some workmen were bringing in more packing cases, one of the men was bent intently over his work, hidden by one of these cases.

"Am I disturbing you, my sons?" asked the Pope.

The worker behind the packing case, thinking that he recognized the voice of one of his companions, brusquely replied: "After you stop playing the fool, come over here and give me a hand."

Pope John approached and reached out a hand from the other side of the packing case. Suddenly the worker looked up. Turning deathly pale, he stammered, "Holiness, Holiness . . ."

The Pope blessed him and his companions. Noticing that the worker who had spoken to him so perfunctorily was still deeply embarrassed, he tried to put him at ease:

"You and I belong to the same party."

"But I don't belong to any party," replied the worker.

"Look at the width of my frame," said the Pope. "For people like you and me, membership in the party of the stoutly built is a foregone conclusion."

Thereupon he invited the workers to lunch with him, but they were too awed and barely touched the food. Perceiving their discomfiture, Pope John wished them a hearty appetite and left them to themselves.

(*Extract from* Le Pèlerin.)

MY NOVITIATE

At the beginning of his pontificate, John XXIII found it hard to realize that he had become Pope and felt ill at ease in his new office. "I'm about to begin my novitiate," he said of himself. And he added: "In the first days of this pontificate I did not fully realize what it means to be the Bishop of Rome, and therefore the pastor of the universal Church. Then, week after week, the light dawned fuller and fuller. And I felt very much at home, as though I had done nothing else during my whole life!"

THE POPE AND THE MURDERER

During a visit to the Regina Cœli prison in Rome, the Pope requested that the inmates be allowed to leave their cells so that he might address them in the main courtyard of the prison. In the course of this speech he did not hesitate to recall that one of his cousins had once been arrested for poaching and had served a stretch in jail.

The Pope expressed pleasure at this opportunity to visit these incarcerated thieves, murderers, seducers. "I have come," he said, "you have seen me. I have looked into your eyes, I have placed my heart alongside your hearts. Be assured that this meeting will remain deeply engraved in my heart."

Among the prisoners who were allowed to approach the Pope, there were two murderers. One of them, after kissing the Pontiff's ring, looked up at him with deep sadness on his face. "Are those words of hope you have given us meant for such a great sinner as I am?"

In response the Pope bent over the convict and embraced him.

⚜✦⟡✦⚜✦⟡✦⚜

One of the prisoners had drawn a picture of the Pope and had intended to present it to him at an opportune moment. But the guards intervened when he tried to do so. As Pope John passed in front of his cell, the prisoner again showed him his work, but still the Pontiff did not understand that it was supposed to be a gift for him. On the following day the newspapers reported the incident and the prisoner's distress. John XXIII immediately dispatched a prelate to pick up the picture with instructions to extend his apologies to the prisoner for the grief he had unwittingly caused him.

An equally touching detail, deserving mention in this connection, is that the Pope used two missals only in celebrating his Mass: one had been presented to him by the inmates of Melun; the other was a gift from the convicts of Regina Cœli.

THE GOOD EMPLOYER

Immediately after his enthronement, Pope John granted considerable salary increases to the employees of Vatican City, beginning with those in the lowest brackets. Thus an usher now earns a salary of 70,000 Lire per month, plus a sum of 12,500 Lire for each child, plus 10,000 Lire allowance for his wife, in addition to an extra month's pay each year. The cardinals saw their stipend set at 400,000 Lire a month.

A prelate who was of the opinion that the increases in the lower brackets were exaggerated, respectfully pointed out to Pope John that they would constitute a big addition to the pontifical budget.

To tease him, Pope John replied:

"Not only have we increased the stipends of the functionaries in the lowest brackets, but we have further decreased the stipends of those in the higher brackets. Thus I foresee a savings of about twenty million per month for our treasury . . ."

A SEMINARIAN UNDER PUNISHMENT

John XXIII detested solitude, particularly during meals. Although protocol requires that a pope dine alone, he could not resign himself to the rule. "I look like a seminarian under punishment," complained the Pope.

Again he declared: "I have read the Gospel over carefully without finding a single passage which prescribes that one should eat alone. As we know, Jesus loved to eat in company."

DRESSED LIKE A SATRAP

Pope John was irked by pontifical pomp and had a horror of official ceremonies and the complications of certain adornments of pontifical vestments. Nor did he scruple to say so: "I'm dressed up like a Persian satrap!"

NO CAUSE FOR SCANDAL

Formerly, the public had been forbidden access to the cupola of St. Peter's so that people might not see the Pope as he took his stroll through the Vatican Gardens. John XXIII had this restriction lifted, declaring: "But why can't the faithful watch me? I don't do anything that would give cause for scandal . . ."

WHO GOVERNS THE CHURCH?

Pope John confessed that he had some difficulty in falling asleep on the night of the memorable day that he announced the convocation of Vatican Council II. He said that he talked to himself in this way:

"Giovanni, why don't you sleep? Is it the Pope or the Holy Spirit who governs the Church? It's the Holy Spirit, no? Well, then, go to sleep, Giovanni!"

3

CHARACTERISTICS

༈༺༈༻༈༺༈

HOSPITALITY

"Wherever I may go in the world, anyone from Bulgaria who might be in distress and who comes to my house at night will find a candle lit in my window. He has only to knock, and the door will be opened to him, whether he be Catholic or Orthodox. 'A brother from Bulgaria,' this will be title enough. He will find the most affectionate hospitality."

(Farewell address in Sophia.)

• *49*

THE MADMAN

As Nuncio to Turkey, Msgr. Roncalli had no desire for a change, and felt himself unfitted for the difficult and delicate mission to Paris. Upon learning that the appointment had been confirmed, he regretfully departed for Rome. When, upon his arrival at the Vatican, someone expressed surprise at his lack of enthusiasm for his new post, he burst out:

"Who's the madman who is sending me there?"

What was his embarrassment to learn that the "madman" was none other than Pope Pius XII!

SOCIETY DINNERS

The prospect of living in Paris and participating in the elegance and worldliness of its social life held little attraction for Msgr. Roncalli. After his appointment, he left Rome in a black cassock which was so much too tight for him that later he had to change into the civilian attire which he usually wore in the Near East. Before boarding the plane, an army Junker, he murmured:

"Just one look at me and anyone would know there is nobody less suited than I for the apostolate of dinner parties."

THE NUNCIO
AND THE SOVIET AMBASSADOR

As soon as he arrived in Paris, on December 30, 1944, Msgr. Roncalli hurried to see the Soviet ambassador who, in the absence of a representative of the Holy See, was ready to extend the New Year greetings of the diplomatic corps to General Charles de Gaulle, President of the Provisional Government. Since by tradition the Apostolic Nuncio is the dean of the corps, Msgr. Roncalli proposed that he be allowed to read the speech which the Russian had prepared. The Soviet ambassador graciously agreed and showed the Nuncio what he had written.

After reading the Russian's speech, the Nuncio said: "I see nothing that should be changed in the text, Excellency, apart from the addition of a brief reference to Providence. I am sure that you will have no objection if I read this in your stead. It will be an excellent beginning to our diplomatic collaboration."

And this was done.

FEET ON THE GROUND

Msgr. Roncalli was tremendously fond of La Fontaine and quoted his fables even in speeches of the most official character which he delivered in Paris. He knew whole verses by heart. And if anyone expressed surprise at this enthusiasm, he would say:

"I know that La Fontaine is not very Catholic. Sometime even his morality is contestable. But he does teach us to walk with our two feet on the ground."

But another time he said:

"We all like to judge events from the vantage point of the handful of earth beneath our feet. This is a great illusion. We must take our view from the heights and courageously embrace the whole."

THE NUNCIO AND DE GAULLE

The Nuncio in Paris was host to the Cardinal-Archbishop of Rennes when, in January 1946, there came the announcement of the resignation of General de Gaulle. All those present were visibly upset, but the Nuncio's composure was not disturbed, and he let drop the arch remark:

"Believe me, no man is irreplaceable."

It must be admitted that at that time the Nuncio entertained no special fondness for General de Gaulle, whose government had slandered his predecessor, Cardinal Valerio Valeri. Moreover, it had demanded the replacement of about thirty bishops labeled as "collaborators." Msgr. Roncalli let things drag along, and in the end there were only three departures. "I removed a zero," he said.

However, after becoming Pope, John XXIII opined: "When I was in Paris, De Gaulle and I were not always in agreement. But now We feel that he is right."

DON CAMILLO
AND VINCENT AURIOL

Msgr. Roncalli felt a great friendship for President Vincent Auriol, a Socialist, and this friendship was to endure. Later, as Patriarch of Venice, he received him cordially—to the great scandal of narrow-minded persons of his diocese. One day in Paris he presented the President with a gift, a copy of the book, *The Little World of Don Camillo*. By way of dedication, he wrote:

"For his amusement and spiritual delight.

"A. Roncalli, Nuncio"

IMPROVING WITH AGE

During an official dinner in Paris at the residence of President Herriot, Msgr. Roncalli startled the old political leader by quoting to him passages from the radical theorist Léon Bourgeois. When the Mayor of Lyons expressed astonishment at the Nuncio's familiarity with this writer, Msgr. Roncalli replied: "Well! What does separate us? Our ideas . . . Admit that this is a trifling matter!"

On another occasion—they were in the company of oldsters—Herriot darted this barbed question at him: "Do you believe, *mon cher* Roncalli, that men improve as they grow older?"

"That depends!" replied Msgr. Roncalli. "In this respect men are like wines. Age improves some of them!"

STOUT AS I AM

John XXIII was the first to joke about his corpulence. On one occasion, pointing to his own plumpness, he said to Herriot: "Look! we're from the same *arrondissement!*" *

✦✳❧✦✳❧✦✳

When, in 1957, Cardinal Roncalli went to Riese, birthplace of Pius X, to unveil a bust of Cardinal Monico, he was applauded by an enthusiastic crowd. Among the cheers, voices were heard shouting: "He's Pius X come back again! *Viva* Pius X!"

"Pius X indeed!" protested the future Pope John XXIII. "Stout as I am, I don't even resemble him physically. Besides, he was a saint!"

✦✳❧✦✳❧✦✳

The first time Msgr. Roncalli received the wraithlike Daniel-Rops at the nunciature, sighing deeply, he said to him: "Ah, *cher monsieur* Daniel-Rops, we will both have to say a prayer to God, beseeching Him to remove half the excess fat which I have and to give it to you!"

✦✳❧✦✳❧✦✳

The Nuncio once attended a solemn meeting of the French Academy. At the end, he commented:

* *Arrondissement:* in France a district, section or territory "rounded off" for electoral or administrative purposes. *Tr.*

"It's a beautiful, most impressive place. One hears beautiful things there. Unfortunately, the seats are large enough only for a demi-nuncio."

A GLASS OF WINE

No worker could come to make repairs at the nunciature in Paris without being invited to drink a glass of wine with the future Pope John XXIII. There was even an Italian welder, named Giuseppe, whose custom it was to have dinner with the Nuncio on the first Saturday of each month, to which he would also bring his wife and his seven *bambini*.

Neither was it a rare sight to see Msgr. Roncalli share the modest repasts of UN officials in the UNESCO canteen on Avenue Kléber after his appointment as the Holy See's permanent observer to UNESCO in 1952.

Later in Venice, during the summertime, the Patriarch could occasionally be seen unobtrusively sipping a glass of white wine in one of the city's cafés near St. Mark's Square.

NO FUN TO WORK
SO NEAR THE BOSS

Before leaving Paris the new Cardinal still had no idea that he was going to be appointed to the post in Venice. Instead, he was afraid that he might be assigned to the Roman Curia. When someone expressed surprise over this excessive trepidation, he broke into a smile.

"Believe me," he said, "it's no fun to go back and work so near the boss!"

DIZZINESS

The rounds of applause in St. Peter's that followed his utterances displeased John XXIII. He hit upon an effective way to cut down their frequency by ordering that the *Credo* be intoned the moment he had finished speaking.

→米→۞→米→۞→米

The *sedia gestatoria* was infinitely distasteful to him. The efforts of the bearers to balance this sedan chair made him dizzy. Consequently he rarely used it and then only in order to give the faithful at a distance a chance to get a glimpse of him as he passed by.

"This is the most uncomfortable chair I know!" protested Pope John.

→米→۞→米→۞→米

"The Pope is a prisoner in his great palaces," confided John XXIII one day to the peasants of an Italian village.

→米→۞→米→۞→米

One morning as he watched the Master of the Chamber, the Prefect of Ceremonies and the Commander of the Gendarmerie successively fussing around him, Pope John exploded: "Behold my prison guards!"

SERGEANT RONCALLI

During an audience John XXIII recognized Reverend Father Pignatello, chaplain general of the Italian army, under whom he had served in the First World War when he was simply Father Roncalli.

The chaplain knelt to kiss the papal ring. After receiving this homage, Pope John drew himself up at attention, executed a smart salute and, smiling mischievously, reported:

"Sergeant Roncalli, at your orders, General!"

"I'VE GOT TO GET HOME"

Pope John continued to express himself as though he were just another man like all the others, as he had in all humility assured the welcoming throng in Venice. Thus at the end of a visit, when he was in a hurry to return to the Vatican, he said:

"I'm late. I've got to get home."

COUNT RONCALLI

A personage at the Roman court one day suggested to the newly elected Pontiff that he bestow titles of nobility upon his brothers.

Pope John cut him short: "What titles shall I give them?"

"Most Holy Father, those of count, marquis or prince . . ."

John XXIII was seized by a fit of laughter. "Imagine my brothers in tuxedoes and with decorations! Besides," he added with a broad smile, "they are close to becoming counts since they already are *contadini* (peasants)!"

Thereupon Pope John related the following story: One day, during his nunciature in Paris, his brothers, Alfredo and Severo, bought themselves black suits in order to attend a solemn official ceremony. Neither of the two knew how to knot his tie, and in despair they had turned to him for assistance. The Nuncio, equally unable to perform such a task, summoned his secretary who also turned out to be hopelessly incompetent. Finally it was the nunciature's chauffeur who managed to complete the job of decking his brothers out in formal attire.

↗✳↘◉↗✳↘◉↗✳

There was a gentleman residing in Rome who went by the name of Count Roncalli. Upon being asked whether this personage might be a kinsman, Pope John replied:

"Maybe he's my cousin, but he's certainly not the cousin of my brothers!"

VISIONS

Pope John gave an audience to a group of priests in June 1960. During the informal conversation which he had with them, before imparting his blessing, he dropped a remark which left his visitors openmouthed.

"I am not a pope who sees visions. Yet they tell me I'm not doing so badly!"

This did not prevent the Pope from making the following remark during the first session of the Council:

"I would like very much for Our Lord to appear to me to tell me when the Council will end. To get it started, I am in command, but to finish it! ! ! . . .'"

FROM POPE TO POPE

On occasion John XXIII was quite capable of making remarks of an incisive character. Such as one, for example, which obviously in no way denoted a lack of esteem and affection for Cardinal Montini. The latter, as is known, was the prelate to whom Pope John listened most attentively during the Council, so much so, in fact, that a wag has described the Pope's opening address to Vatican II, in the preparation of which Cardinal Montini had collaborated, as "ultra-Montini" and not *ultra-montano* (ultramontane).

During an audience with a prelate who was a member of the entourage of the Archbishop of Milan, now Paul VI, the Pope asked: "How goes it with your Hamlet of a cardinal?"

BANKERS

The Pope told a gathering of Italian bankers:

"I searched through the Gospel for a long time for something that relates to your profession and I didn't find a thing. But suddenly"—here the Pontiff tapped his forehead—"I remembered that there was something even for you."

And Pope John recounted to the gathering of financiers the Gospel parable of the talents.

A BACHELOR? JUST LIKE ME!

One day an Asiatic ambassador was received in audience. Pope John walked up to him and began to chat familiarly, as was his habit. He inquired about the diplomat's family. At this point the guest interrupted the Pope, saying: "I'm not married, Holy Father."

"Ah, so you're a bachelor! Just like me!" exclaimed the Pope.

"Not exactly, Holy Father," replied the ambassador honestly.

NOTHING TO DO

During an audience with another ambassador, John XXIII confided: "I have nothing to do any more since I have become Pope. My bureaus take things off my shoulders. Now I sleep peacefully, whereas in Venice I often got up in the middle of the night to work."

A GOOD DIPLOMAT

"In order to be a good diplomat," said the Pope, "there are only two possible solutions: either one must be as mute as a mole, or garrulous to the point where one's proposals lose any importance. Given the fact that I am an Italian, I prefer the second method."

Faithful to this principle, it is said that John XXIII never stopped talking when he received a visitor who he knew was going to request a favor which would be impossible to grant. Thus the visitor, unable to get in a word, would depart without having been given a chance to formulate the request which had been the original purpose of his coming.

A TALKATIVE PERSON

John XXIII was incorrigibly talkative. He knew it and often made fun of himself for this minor Italianate fault.

Yet, at the beginning of his pontificate, upon being asked whether he planned to increase the promulgation of encyclicals and addresses as his predecessor had done, he replied:

"I shall talk much less, but I shall say as much!"

⁎⁎⁎⁎⁎⁎⁎⁎⁎

"My speech was a trifle too long, but it certainly responded to that mysterious something overhead and, perhaps, it stirred some hearts."

(An entry in his diary in reference
to the canonization of St. Vincent Pallotti,
January 1963.)

MUTE

During a public audience, John XXIII passed before a group of persons whom he did not identify. "UNESCO, UNESCO," Monsignor Callori di Vignali whispered to him over and over again. But the Pontiff's thoughts seemed to be elsewhere. Suddenly he stopped in his tracks and, before the startled crowd, repeatedly began to touch his chest, his forehead and finally his lips.

Then he explained: "The words are here in my heart, in my head, but they do not come to my lips."

ST. PAUL'S INDEX FINGER

One of Pope John's principles regarding governance of the Church was that one should not give orders if one were not morally certain they would be executed. By way of illustration, he commented on the significance of the statues of Sts. Peter and Paul on the Piazza Bernini.

"The former points the index finger of his right hand towards the ground. This means: 'It is here that laws are made.' The latter points his index finger towards the horizon. This means: 'It is out there, in the distance, that they are applied.'"

INDISCREET MICROPHONES

On Easter Sunday, the crowd which had gathered in St. Peter's Square to receive the papal benediction was surprised to hear the Pope, who was standing in front of the window which had just been opened, utter these words:

"There's an awful draft!"

✦✱✦☮✦✱✦☮✦✱

At the general audience, the Pope had to address a group of Britons in English, a language which he spoke poorly. He spluttered out some words and soon got hopelessly tangled up. Thereupon he ordered a prelate to extend his apologies and to tell his visitors that he was learning English, and that the next time they came he would deliver a more satisfactory talk. Then the Pope, thinking that the microphones had been switched off, turned to a prelate standing beside him and muttered: *"Basta!* if they think I'm going to learn English, they can wait for ever and a day!"

Yet John XXIII did take English lessons during the pontificate.

WE DON'T HAVE TROUBLE WITH OUR LIVER

"I am not so much a man of principles as I am a practical and balanced man."[1]

"We don't have trouble with our liver, thank God, nor

[1] It often happened that the Pope forgot or refused, even in circumstances of great solemnity, to use the pontifical "We."

any trouble with our nerves. This is why we like company and enjoy being among people."

THE MOST BEAUTIFUL AGE

"Sixty years old! It is the most beautiful age! Good health, in addition good sense, a happy disposition to see things more clearly, with kindness, optimism and trust."

꙳꙳꙳꙳꙳꙳꙳

"The contacts with the crowds, the audiences, oh, what consolations!"

THE POPE'S POLITENESS

While touring the Vatican Gardens one day, the Pope's automobile nearly struck down a prelate who was a member of the staff of the Vatican Radio Station.

The priest came up to the door of the car and proffered his apologies: "Excuse me, Holiness."

"We should apologize to you," replied Pope John, "another inch and you would have been run over."

I DON'T KNOW ALL THAT

It will be recalled that the encyclical *Mater et magistra* was promulgated after a delay of several weeks. The official reason given, which almost nobody believed, attributed the delay to the time required for trans-

Don Angelo Roncalli
Secretary to Bishop Radini-Tedeschi

Sotto il Monte, Birthplace of Angelo Roncalli

Room in which he was born

Giovanni Battista Roncalli
Father of Angelo Roncalli

Angelo Roncalli (center)
as student in
Roman Seminary (1901)

Bishop Radini-Tedeschi of Bergamo

Chaplain Roncalli with his two brothers during World War I

lating it into several languages. Actually it is believed that the Pope was not pleased with the first version presented to him and that it was necessary to rewrite the encyclical.

Pope John had protested. "But it's much too complicated! My faithful surely know that I don't know all that. Write the text over again, more succinctly, more simply, and make it less technical. Above all make it more concrete."

WOULD I HAVE PULLED A LONG FACE?

When a bishop, in his presence, expressed surprise that the Pope had not presided personally over the first session of the Council, John XXIII retorted:

"But my sphere of my jurisdiction is not universal. Besides, had I been there, would you have felt so free? For instance, would you have had the courage to applaud when the chairman interrupted Cardinal Ottaviani during his intervention? And if you would have displayed the courage, you all would have looked at me to see the kind of face I would have pulled. Isn't that so?"

4
HUMOR

✦✲✦✦✲✦✦✲✦✲✦

THE CONCLAVE

Walking through the streets of Rome one day, Pope
John heard a woman, taken aback by the Pope's obesity,
make the remark to her companion: "God, but he's fat!"

Pope John turned around and benignly observed:
"But Madame, you must know that the conclave is not
exactly a beauty contest!"

KNEELING BENCHES AT
THE ACADEMY

The Association of French Catholic Writers gave a grand luncheon on the occasion of the election of Daniel-Rops to the French Academy. Msgr. Roncalli had the final word, saying:

"If this continues, the French Academy will not be needing armchairs but kneeling benches!"

ACCENTS

At the end of a banquet in Paris, the Nuncio recited a fable by La Fontaine in his picturesque Italian accent. Following the polite round of applause, Vincent Auriol leaned towards him and in his thick accent of the Muret region said urbanely: "If I have correctly understood, that must have been La Fontaine."

Msgr. Roncalli, with equal urbanity retorted: "Ah, now I understand you, *Monsieur le President*. It took me just as long a time to get used to *your* accent."

THE PELICAN

"The Church is like the pelican . . . She deprives herself of honors in order to confer them on others."

(Words of John XXIII in announcing the elevation to the purple of a cardinal without the Pope's having been responsible for the promotion, as had been supposed.)

70 ·

AH, JACQUELINE!

A few minutes before receiving President and Mrs. Kennedy, Pope John, evincing an air of vague concern, inquired as to the proper mode of addressing the wife of the President of the United States.

"Your Holiness," replied the monsignor in charge of protocol, "can choose either Madame President or simply Madame."

"Ah!" said the Pope with a thoughtful air.

But when John XXIII entered the audience chamber, he spontaneously opened his arms, smiled broadly and exclaimed: "Ah, Jacqueline!"

THE WORKING HALF

A diplomat newly accredited to the Holy See was received by the Pope. He asked the Pontiff how many persons worked at the Vatican.

"Oh, no more than half of them!" replied John XXIII, winking an eye.

TELEVISION

Someone once asked the Pope whether he liked television.

"I should say I do!" he replied. "Ever since, thanks to TV, I saw myself made Pope, I attach a great importance to it."

AT NIGHT

Pope John frequently left the confines of the Vatican and this gave rise to some criticism. In an allusion to this, the Pope declared:

"So they say that I go out too much during the day! Very well, from now on I'll go out at night."

THE VICAR AND THE
MOTHER SUPERIOR

One day John XXIII visited the Hospital of the Holy Spirit in Rome which is administered by a religious sisterhood. The mother superior, deeply stirred by the papal visitation, went up to him in order to introduce herself:

"Most Holy Father, I am the Superior of the Holy Spirit!" she said.

"Well, I must say you're lucky," replied the Pope. "I'm only the Vicar of Jesus Christ!"

DO AS I DO

Msgr. Chevalier, Bishop of Mans, was named to succeed Cardinal Grente in the French Academy. He was telling the Pope how difficult it would be to replace such a personage.

Pope John interrupted him: "But how about me? Do you think it's easy? I'll give you some good advice. Do as I do: 'differently.'"

WHO'S THE POPE?

Pope John had a great appreciation of the intelligence of one of his closest collaborators. One day he said of him:

"He has lots of ideas, but sometimes I wonder who's the Pope—he or I. I let him talk . . ."

5
VARIATIONS

❀✻❀❀✻❀❀✻❀

✦✳✦✿✦✳✦✿✦✳

ABSENT-MINDEDNESS

One evening in 1949, Msgr. Roncalli heard the bell
at the nunciature ring at dinner time. Surprised, he himself went to open the door and found himself face to
face with Francisque Gay, an important member of
the French diplomatic corps. He proffered apologies in
a state of great embarrassment:

"I completely forgot I had given this invitation."

"It makes no difference at all so far as I am con-
cerned," replied Francisque Gay. "But Your Excellency
also invited one of the directors of UNRA and, I believe, a Brazilian bishop as well."

"It's terrible! And my housekeeper isn't here! Come, let's get a move on. Let's go to the kitchen right away and throw something together."

When the bishop arrived, Francisque Gay, wearing an apron under his white goatee, opened the door for him. Finally all the invited guests were gathered in the kitchen around the stove where Msgr. Roncalli was busy making a *polenta*.

"Isn't this the best thing in the world that one can eat?" asked the Nuncio. "Back home they call it the 'Lord's dish.' They call it that because you can always find a little cornmeal and a drop of olive oil in any house, no matter how poor it might be."

✦✳✦⊕✦✳✦⊕✦✳

John XXIII recounted that in the first months of his pontificate he often awoke during the night, thinking himself still a cardinal and worried over a difficult decision to be made.

At these times, he said, he would say to himself: "I'll talk it over with the Pope!"

Then he would remember where he was.

"But *I'm* the Pope!" he would say to himself. After which he would conclude: "Well, I'll talk it over with Our Lord!"

THE POPE VANISHES

One morning at six o'clock, Monsignor Capovilla, Pope John's secretary, came to knock at the door of the Holy Father's small private apartment at Castel Gandolfo. There was no answer. He went to the chapel. Nobody there. Amazed, the secretary telephoned several persons to ask if they had seen the Pope. Nobody had. So Monsignor Capovilla alerted the cardinals present in the summer residence, the gendarmerie, and the Swiss Guards. Searches were conducted with no result. Someone suggested that the Italian police be notified. Cardinal Canali advised waiting so as not to alarm anyone unnecessarily.

Finally a young member of the Swiss Guard discovered John XXIII sitting in a thicket in the park—peacefully reading.

When he realized that so many people had been looking for him, the Pope apologized:

"The morning was so beautiful and We were not sleepy. So We got up without disturbing anyone and took a little walk. . . ."

THE POPE'S REPRIMANDS

When a group of pilgrims from his native Bergamo came to Rome, a notable of Sotto il Monte made so bold as to address John XXIII as follows:

"To be sure, the village in which Your Holiness was born still lacks many comforts. The pilgrims who come are inconvenienced. For example, we have no macadam roads. It would be enough, surely, just to drop a word to some of the higher-ups."

The Pope smiled and said: "As you know, there are

two authorities in this world: God and Caesar. That they get along together is a magnificent thing, and it fills me with joy. But that they should begin to practice '*do ut des*' (I give so that you give), well, that's something that the Pope cannot allow."

↗※↩☯↗※↩☯↗※

At an audience granted to journalists during General de Gaulle's visit to Rome, a reporter took the liberty of asking the Pope for a summary of his conversation with the President of the French Republic.

Pope John replied in substance: "Young man, you must be quite new at your profession not to know that one does not interrogate the Pope. It is the Pope who does the interrogating."

But toward the end of the audience, not wishing to leave the indiscreet journalist in a state of embarrassment, John XXIII went up and engaged him for a while in cordial conversation.

THE POPE LOSES HIS TEMPER

An obsequious Italian journalist remained stubbornly on his knees while the Pope was giving him some instructions.

"Get up now and sit down on this chair."

"Holy Father, I am quite comfortable on my knees. I am used to a position which I always took in the presence of your predecessors."

"It's proper to pray on your knees but not to work."

When the journalist nevertheless continued to kneel, Pope John sternly ordered:

"Get up and sit down! If you don't get off your knees, I shall leave the room."

↗✳↙☉↗✳↙☉↗✳

At the time Msgr. Roncalli was Apostolic Delegate to Greece, Athens was in the grip of the terrible famine which struck the city during the first year of the war. Corpses were picked up from the streets by the hundreds.

Msgr. Roncalli organized a crash program of assistance. One day Father Leibel, a Capuchin who had opened up an emergency relief center for the starving, indignantly pointed out to him that a certain Athenian merchant was selling flour and dried vegetables at exorbitant prices. Accompanied by his secretary, the future Pope forced open the warehouse door behind which this scoundrel had locked himself and did not hesitate to threaten him with physical violence in order to force him to sell his merchandise at more honest prices.

6

FAVORITE MAXIMS

✻✢✿✣✻✢✿✣✻

"Obedience and peace."
Of this motto on his episcopal coat-of-arms, he said:
"There lies the secret of my successes."

✻✢✿✣✻✢✿✣✻

"Listen to everything, forget much, correct little."

✻✢✿✣✻✢✿✣✻

"*Gutta cavat lapidem*" (Drops of water hollow out a
stone).

✻✢✿✣✻✢✿✣✻

· *85*

"Time must be left to time."

⁕✢⊗✢⁕✢⊗✢⁕

"Let us look at each other without mistrust, meet each other without fear, talk with each other without surrendering principle."

⁕✢⊗✢⁕✢⊗✢⁕

"Unity in necessary things, freedom in doubtful things, charity in all things."

⁕✢⊗✢⁕✢⊗✢⁕

"Give all, but without expectation or hope of recompense."

7

THE DAUGHTERS OF EVE

✤✻✦✛✤✻✦✛✤✻

THE YOUNG VENETIAN

Concrete personal cases were of much greater interest to John XXIII than were ideas of a general character. His concern for others, in their sorrows as well
as in their joys, was proverbial. An excellent memory
served him well in this respect.

When he was Patriarch of Venice, he learned that a
young girl belonging to his diocese had fallen in love
with a French truck driver during her summer holidays
on the Lido beach.

The young man had departed without leaving his address. After waiting in vain for news from him, the girl became ill from grief. Msgr. Roncalli did not hesitate to write to a scout chaplain in Paris to tell him about this and request him to trace this "blonde lad with blue eyes."

The truck driver was found, but the story did not have a happy ending. He was already betrothed to someone else.

UNTIMELY CHATTER

A group of militant ladies belonging to a Catholic Action group were buzzing with excited chatter when the Pope arrived in the audience chamber. His entrance failed to tone them down, so he reprimanded them in these terms:

"It's easy to see that we have with us many daughters of Eve who make themselves noticeable by inability to control their tongues. I shall try to speak louder."

And when the militant ladies continued their chatter, he said: "If you don't keep quiet, I shall be obliged to bless you immediately and to retire to my apartment."

✦❋❖✦❋✦❖✦❋

One day, in a working-class parish, John XXIII commented upon the incident of the "Finding of Jesus in the Temple."

"Joseph had not spoken, he was a man. But Mary told all. She was a woman and women are always talkative."

THE APPLE

Once at a banquet the Apostolic Nuncio to France found himself seated next to an elegant lady in a dress cut overgenerously low in the neck. When dessert was served, he invited her to take the apple which he held out to her. Since the lady showed surprise at this gesture, Msgr. Roncalli added:

"Do take it, Madame, please do. It was only after Eve ate the apple that she became aware of how little she had on!"

⁂

At another dinner, a guest asked the Nuncio: "Are you embarrassed, Monseigneur, when there are women present who wear very low-necked dresses? It's often a scandal."

"A scandal? Why, no," Msgr. Roncalli replied, "when there's a woman with a plunging neckline, the guests don't look at her. They look at the Apostolic Nuncio to see how he is taking it . . ."

8
THE TEMPLE OF CREATION

✦❊↝✿✦❊↝✿✦❊↝✿✦❊

Everything connected with nature, the earth, the sea, animals, flowers, deeply stirred this son of peasants who had spent his childhood in the country.

As a young boy, he had a passion for dogs. He used to make herb gardens. During his vacations as a young seminarian, he sometimes exchanged his cassock for a blue blouse and an old pair of velvet pants and took off on a hike of several days. His family was not surprised to see him come back bespattered with mud and with his hair streaked with grass.

As Nuncio to Sophia, he often went to visit the famous Valley of Roses. In Turkey, he loved to stroll through the magnificent Ghazi Gardens. The floral displays in the Bagatelle Park in Paris had no more faithful admirer than Msgr. Roncalli. M. Meilland, the great breeder of roses, loved to present his latest creations to the Nuncio.

⚶❈❤❀❈❤❀❈

While Patriarch of Venice, he came upon a lovely little abandoned chapel in the course of a trip to Cividavale. He decided to remain there for several hours in order to sketch the broken columns. When his secretary, somewhat amazed at this whim, reminded him of the great amount of work awaiting his attention in Venice, the future Pope retorted:

"But don't you *see* how beautiful it is?"

⚶❈❤❀❈❤❀❈

As Nuncio in Paris, the future John XXIII was fond of betaking himself to the provinces, even for the smallest feasts or celebrations.

"One gets to know France through the *curés'* gardens," was the way he rationalized this keen bent for traveling about. For this very thing he was reprimanded by Pius XII who was of the opinion that the Nuncio should stick more closely to his Paris residence.

⚶❈❤❀❈❤❀❈

"Silence and peace! What a difference between the continual hustle and bustle of Paris and this solitude!

Archbishop Roncalli
Apostolic Visitor to Bulgaria (1927)

1. gennaio 1945

Nuncio in Paris arriving to present credentials

Papal Nuncio presenting New Year's greetings to General De Gaulle

Nuncio Roncalli and Edouard Herriot,
ex-Premier of France

Arrival in Venice as Cardinal Patriarch, March 1953

The Patriarch of Venice congratulates regatta winner (1957)

My spirit is at rest here. From this window, where so many prelates have looked out on the small lake—which was so rough last evening and again last night, but now lies calm in an unsettled morning—it is beautiful to ponder, as they did, the fluctuations of life as such and also of life in the service of Holy Church."

(Retreat at Hautecombe, 1948.)

✦❋✧⊛❋✧⊛❋✦

After becoming Pope, John XXIII was to continue as much as possible—too rarely for his liking—his outings far beyond the hubbub of the city. He would set out alone to recite his breviary on the road, dressed in black like an ordinary parish priest in order to escape being noticed.

He often felt a desire to make long trips within Italy proper and even abroad. He had been on pilgrimages to Lourdes more than ten times.

A few days before his death, he made the following entry in his private diary: "I cannot think of my journey to Loretto and Assisi without deep emotion. . . . I wanted so much to go to Monte Cassino and who knows? Who knows?"

✦❋✧⊛❋✧⊛❋✦

One day, coming upon gardeners at work during his stroll through the Vatican Gardens, Pope John called out to them:

"What a beautiful occupation you have, my sons!"

"Here everything hymns the glory of the Creator and the beauty of His work."

(*On the high seas.*)

❖✳❖❖✳❖✳❖✳❖✳

"If God created shadows it was in order to better emphasize the light."

❖✳❖❖✳❖✳❖✳❖✳

"When the root is healthy, the tree grows vigorously, even in stony soil."

❖✳❖❖✳❖✳❖✳❖✳

"It is easy to see how noble is the work of peasants: they live in the majestic temple of creation. They are in frequent contact with the animal world, inexhaustible in its manifestations, inflexible in its laws, which ceaselessly evoke the Providence of God, the Creator."

❖✳❖❖✳❖✳❖✳❖✳

Once somebody asked Pope John what he would like to do after the Council had finished its labors.

He replied: "Spend a whole day tilling the fields with my brothers!"

THE POPE AND THE LION

Having promised an audience to the members of a traveling circus, Pope John paid a visit to the menagerie.

His eyes fell on a lion cub and he asked its name.

"Dolly," replied one of the circus troupe.

Thereupon the Pope patted the lion cub's head for a long time, and admonished it in these words: "I hope that you will behave properly in Italy. Here we are used every day to the serenity of the lion on the Square of St. Mark."

THE VALUABLE CROCODILE SKINS

In a pastoral letter written during the International Film Festival of 1958, Pope John commented on the summer clothing worn by tourists as follows:

"I do not ask tourists to come to Italy wrapped in furs or woolen garments. They can dress in that cool, light, modern American silk which is a veritable low-priced refrigerator. Italy after all is not below the Equator and, for that matter, even at the Equator lions wear their coats and crocodiles are protected by their valuable skins . . ."

9

BLESSED ARE THE POOR

✣✳✤✤✳✤✤✳✣

✣✣✣✣✣✣✣

A PRISONER DE LUXE

"Having come from the poverty and simplicity of Sotto il Monte, I have never tried to cut myself off from it. How great the grace which the Lord has granted me . . . a felicitous and untroubled poverty. I want to die without knowing whether I have anything that belongs to me. Poverty has often inconvenienced me, especially when I was unable to help my relatives who were very poor, or certain colleagues. But I have never complained about it. Blessed are the poor!"

"Our Giuseppino is right when he tells his brother the Pope: 'You are here a prisoner de luxe who cannot do everything that he would like to do.'"

THE TRUE TITLE OF NOBILITY

"I know very well that you will have to endure some mortifications from those who like to indulge in twaddle: saying that you have a pope in the family upon whom the whole world gazes with respect but who lets his relatives live in such modest circumstances and does nothing to raise their status in society. . . .

"The honor of a pope does not lie in enriching his relatives, but only in assisting them charitably according to their needs. Such is and such will be one of the loftiest and most esteemed honorary titles of Pope John and of the Roncalli family. At my death they will bestow upon me the praise that so greatly honored His Holiness Pius X: 'Born poor and died poor . . .'"

(*Spiritual testament, "To the Roncalli family."*)

✦✲✦☀✲✦☀✲✦☀✦✲

"The appearance of affluence has often veiled the hidden thorns of a painful poverty. I thank God for this grace of poverty to which I vowed myself in my youth: poverty of spirit as a priest of the Sacred Heart, and real poverty. It sustained me in my resolve never to ask for anything, neither for posts, nor for money, nor for favors—never—either for myself, or for my relatives or for my friends.

"I have never had to blush for my blood-relatives because of their simplicity and modesty. This is their true title of nobility. I have helped them sometimes in their most urgent needs, as a poor man helps the poor, but without removing them from the poverty which is their happiness and their joy."

(Testament, 1954.)

AT ASSISI

A journalist who joined the pilgrimage to Assisi, which was decided upon on the spur of the moment on the eve of the Council, wrote the following:

"In my mind's eye I still see him breaking away from the resplendent cortège of beribboned officials with his hurried steps and lumbering gait. Almost stripped of adornment, he mounted the steps of the altar alone. He looked so poor and frail to me when he blessed the feverish throng. Seldom have I understood as at this moment what it means to be a man face to face with God."

(Francis Mayor.)

THE CHURCH OF THE POOR

The poverty of the Church was one of the recurring themes of his pontificate. John XXIII wanted the poor to feel at ease in the Church of Jesus Christ, the poorest of the poor, and he constantly encouraged the Fathers of the Council to take steps in this direction. In his address of September 11, 1962, he took pleasure in quoting this passage of St. Peter in the Acts of the Apostles:

"I have neither gold nor silver, but what I have I give to you."

10

THE SELF-STYLED GREAT
OF THIS WORLD

✦✳✦✦✳✦✦✳✦

✦✳✦✤✦✳✦✤✦✳✦

"I have a dignity which I do not merit and the power of Orders which I cannot even exercise as does a simple priest. I rarely have an opportunity to deliver a spiritual exhortation, I never hear confessions. All day long —in a beautiful house now—I am busy over my typewriter or engaged in tiresome conversations; among many difficulties and thorns, among people who belong to Jesus Christ and by right to the Catholic Church, but who have nothing of the sense of Christ and even less of the *sensus ecclesiae*. I am always in contact with the so-called great of this world, but distressed by the pettiness of their minds in regard to the supernatural."

(*Nunciature in Sophia.*)

· *109*

"I have asked the new recruits of the Swiss Guard to come and have a drink with me this afternoon so that we could get to know each other."

⁺✳⁺⊗⁺✳⁺⊗⁺✳

"This morning I must receive cardinals, princes and important representatives of the Government. But in the afternoon I want to spend a few minutes with some ordinary people who have no other title save their dignity as human beings and children of God."

(To Maione Roméo, former International President of the Jocists.)

11
THE WORLD'S TWADDLE

THE MOST RIDICULOUS OF
CREATURES

"We are made for the splendor of celestial glory. If the Lord also reserves for us a little honor on earth, this is of no value at all and perishes quickly if it is not of God. If the Lord, on the contrary, disposes that the value of our life be entirely hidden in Him it would be ridiculous to look for anything else. The ambitious are the most ridiculous and the most pitiful creatures on the earth."

TO A NEW MONSIGNOR

"As the years multiply, these personal distinctions fade before the loftier dignity which the service of a well-conducted priestly life renders to the Church of the Lord. The *splendor animarum* surpasses the *honor vestium.* But they are things which go well together. To know how to receive them and to know how to make use of them with simplicity and with grace, without excessive cringes of humility as also without 'self-complacency,' delights everybody and edifies both one's brother priests and the Christian people."

✦*✦❀✦*✦❀✦*

"You do well to remain humble as I myself strive to do, and not to be enticed by the flatteries and the twaddle of the world. The worldly delight only in making money, in enjoying life and in imposing themselves on others at any price even if, unhappily, they must behave ruthlessly."

(Spiritual testament, "To the Roncalli family.")

DISTRESSING COLLEAGUES

The pettiness, the vanity of certain "colleagues," their lack of a sense of the supernatural, shocked Pope John. He held these faults responsible for many of the evils in the Church, and for many of her failures. On February 19, 1963, he made the following declaration to the Italian clergy:

"Oh, how distressing it sometimes is to live with certain colleagues who always talk only of the outer forms of priestly activity, who find it hard to repress in their hearts the thirst and pursuit, not always veiled nor modest, for promotions, advancements, distinctions; and who are wont to interpret everything in a minor key, thereby preparing a premature, dreary and irksome old age for themselves!"

12

WAR: A CONTRADICTION

"PACEM IN TERRIS"

"The talk of war is still serious. It will be a slaughter which will end in a universal act of expiation. But oh, what sorrow for so many mothers, wives and innocent creatures!"

"War is a frightful danger. For a Christian who believes in Jesus and His Gospel, it is an iniquity and a contradiction."

(*1940.*)

· *119*

"I shall never be able to forget the screams of an Austrian whose chest was torn apart by a bayonet during the war and who was carried to the hospital at Caporetto where I was an attendant. His image became ever more vivid within me as I worked on the encyclical *Pacem in terris.*"

✦✸✦✿✦✸✦✿✦✸✦

"What a response to *Pacem in terris!* What there is of myself in this document is above all the humble example of the 'peaceful and patient man' (Imitation of Christ, II, 3) which I have tried to set during the whole of my poor life.

"The world has awakened. Little by little, the very pure teaching of the Gospel will find entry into consciences."

(Personal thoughts.)

13

COMMUNISTS

❧✻↣✿❧✻↣✿❧✻

DAVID AND GOLIATH

Concerning Communists, the Pope observed: "They are the enemies of the Church, but the Church has no enemies . . ."

"A little less politics and a little more Christian fervor would be enough to assure vitality and effectiveness to the apostolate," the future Pope wrote in 1947 to the Bishop of Bergamo. One of his key ideas was that priests spend too much time in polemics on the ideological plane and not enough in exerting themselves in a positive way for the good of souls. This is how he discussed the Communist peril and the chances of an unarmed Church at grips with the giant Goliath:

"Yes, we are face to face with the giant Goliath, and perhaps we lose too much time in talking, time which might be better employed in praying or in forming good resolutions for the sanctification of our own souls and those of our neighbors. We are face to face with someone who seems awesome. But he is not strong, he is not powerful, because he is the expression of error, of covetousness, of violence. Sometimes we are invaded by misgivings and become fearful at the thought of the morrow. Nevertheless, this giant must succumb before the will, the grace and the mercy of God. Nor must we think that the victory of this Goliath need bring destruction and universal ruin in its wake, because, even at times when he is dominant, there are still souls nourished with the same light as ourselves, and who remain faithful and very close to us and who share the same Christian and apostolic ideal.

"The simplicity of little David who stood face to face with the giant truly represents the holy and blessed Catholic Church. It represents the glorious handful of our athletes advancing in humility and solidarity in their holy enterprises, comforted and exultant at the thought that they are being followed by magnificent ranks and files . . .

"Let the giant step forth with his menaces. Like the

young lad of Bethlehem (David), the children of the Church, religious and laity, will confront him with the might of God."

THE LIGHT OF YOUR EYES

John XXIII granted an audience to *Izvestia* editor Alexis Adzhubei, Khrushchev's son-in-law, who was accompanied by his wife. During the exchange of introductions, the Pope turned to the latter and asked the name of her children.

"Nikita, Alexis and Ivan!" she replied timidly.

"Three beautiful names indeed!" exclaimed the Pope who did not fail to point out that Ivan corresponded to his own name, John.

Then he added: "When you get home, give your children, and particularly Ivan, an affectionate pat on the head for me. The others must not take offense at this seeming favoritism."

In a later colloquy with editor Adzhubei, Pope John, according to Monsignor Capovilla, recalled the Biblical passages on the creation of the world, and commented on them as follows: "The first epoch was that of light: *fiat lux.* We are at present in the first era, that of light: the light of my eyes has met with the light of your eyes. May the Lord assist the progress of good if it so pleases Him."

14
LOVE YOUR ENEMIES

*Pope Pius XII and
Cardinal Roncalli*

*Cardinal Roncalli casts vote
in Italian election of
May 5, 1958*

Papal Conclave, cell of
Cardinal Roncalli

Turn-box for sending
supplies into Conclave

be John XXIII receiving obedience of Cardinals

Cardinal Ruffini and Cardinal Spellman offer their homage

*First blessing to the City and the World
from balcony of St. Peter's*

SWALLOWING INSULTS

Father A. Z. Serrand wrote that the gentleness and patience that marked Pope John's character gave the impression that he magnanimously swallowed the insults that came his way. In the course of his long life he was often misunderstood, suspected and slandered by those in his entourage. He generally accepted these things without complaint, even finding it normal and helpful to his practice of humility to bear his "cross" in silence.

"No, I am not grieved by what is written or said about me," we read in his diary. "It is much too little when we compare it with the tribulations of Jesus, Son of God, throughout His life and on the Cross."

Or again: "I prefer to continue to keep silent, without bitterness, certain that one day this mortification will be an edifying example to others."

꙳✳✦✧✴✦✧✴✳

But sometimes his cup ran over. One day at dawn he called a priest, who was a close friend, and read to him a letter he had just finished writing. It was addressed to a cardinal well-known to be in total disagreement with John XXIII on the so-called "opening to the left." In this letter Pope John, with his customary nobility but with utter frankness, complained about the cardinal's lack of understanding. Was this letter, dashed off under the spur of emotion, ever sent to the personage to whom it was addressed? Only he who received it would be able to answer this question.

꙳✳✦✧✴✦✧✴✳

After the Italian elections, some malicious talkers tried to hold the Pope responsible for the increase in the size of the Communist vote and to criticize him for this or that passage in *Pacem in terris* concerning collaboration with non-Christians. This backbiting was particularly distressing to him because certain of his adversaries claimed that they were in basic agreement with the substance of the encyclical, but that in their opinion it had been a blunder to publish the encyclical before and not after the elections.

"They are in good faith," said Pope John of them, "I pray for them, I love them more than the others. I am fortunate in being able to forget everything quickly."

A GREATER GOOD

King Boris of Bulgaria, in violation of his solemn commitments, had permitted his son to be baptized according to the rites of the Greek Orthodox Church.

On this John XXIII made the following comment: "He deceived me, but we must live in peace and ever seek it. I have the hope that one day an even greater good will issue from this evil. How wretched human life is! I must pray for him."

15

THE PROPHETS OF DOOM

✢✱✤✿✢✱✤✿✢✤✱

OUR EARS ARE SHOCKED

On the most important day of his life—the opening of Vatican Council II on October 11, 1962, before 2,600 Council Fathers—pessimism, lack of faith, disdain for the modern world, foolish nostalgia for the unreturnable past, wrested this famous outburst from Pope John which surprised everyone because of its mordant note:

"In the daily exercise of Our pastoral office Our ears are shocked, much to Our regret, by the voices of persons who, though burning with religious zeal, are not endowed with too much sense of discretion and measure. In these modern times they can see nothing but calamities and ruin. They say that our era, in comparison with past eras, is getting worse, and they behave as though they have learned nothing from history, which is the teacher of life . . . We feel we must declare our total disagreement with these prophets of doom who always foretell catastrophes as though the world were close to its end."

A CHILD

One day Pope John received two distinguished non-Catholic personages and Cardinal Ottaviani's name cropped up during the three-way conversation. Now the Cardinal is undoubtedly a saintly and wholly disinterested priest, full of zeal and self-denial, but his penchant for integralism and his fear that the pure doctrine of the Church is under attack were not shared by the majority of the Council Fathers.

To his visitors Pope John made the following remark to describe this loveable and venerable churchman:

"Cardinal Ottaviani? Why, he's a child!"

16

LET THE LITTLE CHILDREN COME TO ME

✦✳✦✿✦✳✦✿✦✳

GIVE THEM A HUG FOR ME

"Oh, the children, the children! What riches and what a blessing!"

> (*Last sentence of the spiritual testament*
> *"To the Roncalli family."*)

"When you go back to your homes, hug your children for me. Tell them that it is an affectionate embrace from the Pope!"

> (*Address to Romans on the evening of*
> *October 11, 1962.*)

• *139*

Pope John one day attended a reception given in his honor at the Benedictine Abbey of Subiaco. During the ceremony, he gently reprimanded the sponsors of the reception who were vainly trying to prevent children from standing on the benches so that they might get a better view of the Holy Father.

"Leave them alone! Leave them alone!" the Pontiff urged repeatedly.

✧❈✧☯✧❈✧☯✧❈

On another occasion, Pope John asked a child: "What's your name?"

"Arcangelo."

"Oh, poor me! I'm just plain Angelo!"

POPE OR POLICEMAN?

In the first days of his pontificate John XXIII received a letter from a twelve-year-old boy named Bruno. It read:

"My dear Pope: I am undecided. I want to be a policeman or a Pope. What do you think?"

The Pope replied:

"My little Bruno. If you want my opinion, learn how to be a policeman, because that cannot be improvised. As regards being pope, you will see later. Anybody can be pope; the proof of this is that I have become one. If you ever should be in Rome, come to see me. I would be glad to talk all this over with you."

THE LITTLE BLIND BOY

One day Pope John visited the Hospital of Bambino Gesù on the Janiculum Hill and went from ward to ward visiting at the bedsides of the sick children. He smiled at the tiny inhabitants of the world of illness and they smiled back at him. Some children called out to him: *"Papa Giovanni,* come here!" or just simply "Giovanni! Giovanni!"

The Holy Father stopped at the bedside of a boy called Angelo. "Well, so your name is Angelo? I also used to have that name. Then they made me take another."

Pope John could not restrain his tears when he stood before another bed, that of little Carmine Lemma who was blind as the result of meningitis.

"You are the Pope," said the child. "I know it, but I can't see you." An immense sadness came over the child's face. The Pope sat down on the edge of the bed and for a long time held his arm around the little blind boy's shoulders.

(Georges Huber.)

17
SACRED FREEDOM

THE CHILDREN OF GOD

Pope John granted an audience to the Canadian bishops who had come to Rome for the Council. During its course he said to them:

"Do you think that I brought you to Rome so that you should all sing the same psalm like monks in choir?"

✦✳✦✦✳✦✦✳✦

On another occasion, he told the Council Fathers: "Speak up! Be inventive!"

And another time: "When all the bishops are together, then we shall see what will transpire."

"The providential debates of the first session of the Council have let the truth spring forth and allowed the sacred freedom of the children of God as it exists in the Church to show itself before the whole world."

(Closing speech at the Council.)

⋆✳⤙⊗⤙✳⤙⊗⤙✳

"My brothers, let us resist the voice of hate, let us remain faithful to love, to peace, to gentleness. It is thus that we construct or reconstruct, it is thus that we do honor to the law of human progress which is the triumph of freedom, the element of true individual and social well-being."

(Algiers, 1950.)

A REGRETTABLE "MONITUM"

Pope John's sense of freedom and his respect for others did not predispose him to pronouncing condemnations. It is well known that John XXIII had little sympathy for the mentality of certain members of the Holy Office who see heresies everywhere and who believe in the efficacy of the Index or of monitions.

In 1940 Pope John made the following entry in his diary: "To respect their freedom of action is the best means for making men benevolent, devout and docile to good counsels."

Thus several days after the Holy Office had thought

it expedient to publish a *monitum* against Teilhard de Chardin, John XXIII—although he had scant appreciation for the thought of the brilliant Jesuit scholar [1]— did not hesitate to state publicly during an audience that "this measure is regrettable." Obviously the remark was widely spread, and it caused dismay and consternation in the Holy Office, which is presided by the Pope himself.[2]

[1] As Nuncio to Paris, Msgr. Roncalli once said to Father Rouquette: "Couldn't this Teilhard content himself with teaching the cathechism and the social doctrine of the Church, instead of raising all these problems?" (See *Etudes*, July-August 1963.)

[2] The *monitum*, which are simple admonitions and not entries on the Index, do not go through the hands of the Sovereign Pontiff.

18

GOOD AND BAD THEOLOGY

❦❦❦❦❦❦❦

YOU ARE NOT A THEOLOGIAN?

DEO GRATIAS!

"Are you a theologian?" Pope John once asked an eminent non-Catholic churchman.

"No, Holy Father," replied his interlocutor, slightly embarrassed.

"Well, *Deo gratias!* Neither am I, any more than it's necessary to claim. You can see yourself how many misfortunes the professional theologians have inflicted on the Church by their subtleties, their self-love, their narrowness of spirit and their obstinacy!"

But it would be advisable not to take this remark literally as is attested by the following reflection written in 1961 in the course of a retreat:

"In these days I have become familiar with St. Leo the Great and with Innocent III. Unfortunately few ecclesiastics bother to read these Pontiffs who are so rich in theological and pastoral doctrine. I shall never let myself tire of dipping into these precious sources of theological wisdom and of lofty and delightful poetry."

THE ARMS OF MERCY

We have just seen that Pope John had no liking for poor theologians, but he had even less liking for condemnations. In his opening address to the Council, he said:

"Nowadays the Church prefers to use the arms of mercy rather than those of severity."

THIRTY CENTIMETERS OF CONDEMNATIONS

Upon rereading a preparatory schema of the Council which was particularly narrow and hostile in regard to the works of modern theologians and exegetes, Pope John grabbed a ruler and said to one of his close collaborators:

"Look, there are thirty centimeters of condemnation in this schema!"

19

A COUNCIL? FRESH AIR

THE HOLY MOUNTAIN

"Without having reflected on the matter earlier, I mentioned the words council, diocesan synod, and revision of the Code of Canon Law in my first conversation with my Secretary of State on January 20, 1959. Without ever having thought about it, and even contrary to all I could suppose or imagine on this point. . . . The first to be startled by my proposal was myself, and before anyone else had given his reactions. And I might say that later it all appeared so natural to me in its immediate and steady development. After three years of preparation . . . here I am now on the slopes of the holy mountain!"

۞۞۞۞۞۞۞۞۞

"The idea of the Council did not ripen in me as the fruit of long meditation, but came forth like the flower of an unexpected spring."

۞۞۞۞۞۞۞۞۞

"The Council. God knows that I opened my small soul to this great inspiration with the utmost simplicity. Will He grant me enough time to finish it? May He be praised if He does not grant it. . . . I shall see the happy conclusion from heaven where I hope, and am even certain, Divine Mercy will allow me to enter."

(Personal thoughts written down a few months before his death.)

۞۞۞۞۞۞۞۞۞

A prelate of the Curia told the Pope: "It is absolutely impossible to open the Council in 1963."
Pope John replied: "Fine, we'll open it in 1962!"

SHAKE OFF THE IMPERIAL DUST

What did John XXIII expect from the Council? He explained himself profusely on this complex subject.

But one day he made a gesture and uttered words that were eloquent in their Franciscan simplicity.

"The Council?" he said as he moved towards the window and made a gesture as if to open it. "I expect a little fresh air from it. . . ."

"We must shake off the imperial dust that has accumulated on the throne of St. Peter since Constantine."

(To an ambassador.)

AN ACT OF GOODNESS

"Wherever Rome is, one must find maternal goodness. We desire above all that the Council be an act of goodness!"

✧✳✦⊗✧✳✦⊗✧✳

During the public sessions of the Council over which he presided, Pope John insisted that his chair, installed in front of the altar of the Confession, be divested of all the customary characteristics of a throne. In fact, according to his own words, he wanted "to be only a bishop among bishops."

✧✳✦⊗✧✳✦⊗✧✳

"Once the Council has begun, I know well the task that will be reserved for me: to suffer."

(To Cardinal Suenens.)

20

THE CHURCH?
A PUBLIC FOUNTAIN

❀❀❀❀❀

At Mass of Coronation

Cardinal Tardini
Papal Secretary of State

At College of the Propaganda Fide

Pope John XXIII in his study

*Coat-of-arms of
Pope John XXIII*

NEITHER A MUSEUM . . .

"Don't remain motionless like statues in a museum."

(To a lay delegation.)

"We are here on earth not to guard a museum, but to cultivate a garden flourishing with life and promised to a glorious future."

. . . NOR A FORTRESS

"The representatives of the Church do not want to take refuge on an island or lock themselves up in a

fortress. This would be tantamount to neglecting im
mense multitudes, many of whom, without being Christians, nevertheless have an idea of God."

"He is on the wrong path who would limit himself to
contemplating the luminous heavens and who keeps
hidden the treasure that is the truth handed down by
our forefathers."

WATER FOR ALL

"People of all kinds come to my poor fountain. My
function is to give drink to all. To leave a good impression behind, even in the heart of a brigand, seems to
me to be a work of love that in due season will bring
forth a blessing.

"The Church is not an archaeological museum, but
the ancient fountain which slakes the thirst of the
generation of today as she did that of the generations
of the past."

✦✳↴✪✦✳↴✪✦✳

"The bishop is always a public fountain."

✦✳↴✪✦✳↴✪✦✳

"Every parish is my family album."

21
COUNT THE SHEEP
ONE BY ONE

✦✻✦✦✻✦✦✻

THE POLAR STAR
OF MY PRIESTHOOD

Young Don Angelo Roncalli matured in heart and mind during the many years he served as secretary to Msgr. Radini-Tedeschi, Bishop of Bergamo. He ardently admired this prelate who, though a patrician, was greatly solicitous and aware of the needs of the working-class of his time. Bishop Radini-Tedeschi also had his bone to pick with the Curia (one can say that the two resembled each other like brothers). Pope John described him as follows:

"He was the polar star of my priesthood. His soul was more disposed to note merits than to exaggerate faults. He treated everybody with the greatest defer-ence. He spoke with incomparable pleasantness, season-ing his conversation with unexpected witticisms. He was not authoritarian. He wanted all those around him to contribute their energies to the apostolate and to assume their proper responsibilities. He was discreet. One remarked a depth of inexhaustible gaiety in his soul.

" 'Good,' he said, 'must be done properly and well. Good must be gratuitous and not linked to any servitude.' "

A LOYAL AND PEACEFUL PRIEST

"May everyone be able to say of me that I have never sowed dissension and mistrust. That I have never grieved any immortal soul by engendering suspicion or fear; that I have been frank, loyal, trusting; that I have looked into the eyes of others with brotherly sympathy, even into those of persons who do not share my ideas, so as not to hinder the realization, in its season, of the great commandment of Jesus: *Unum sint!* That they be one!"

⁕⁎❖⁕⁎❖⁕⁎

"Oh, how poor the life of the bishop or of the priest who is reduced to being only a diplomat or a bureaucrat!"

⁕⁎❖⁕⁎❖⁕⁎

As is known, it was Vincent Auriol, President of the French Republic, who presented Nuncio Roncalli with his cardinal's red biretta on January 15, 1953. On that occasion the future Pope made the following declaration to the distinguished personages who had gathered in the Elysée Palace to honor him:

"It will be enough for me if every good Frenchman, recalling my name and my sojourn among you, shall be able to say: 'He was a loyal and peaceful priest, always and in all circumstances a sure and sincere friend of France.'"

✢✳✢✣✢✳✢✣✢✳

"If you knew how I blush when I have to speak to my priests!"

A COUNTRY PRIEST

"The priest? From the day I was born, I thought of nothing else than to become a priest. Thus was a humble son of the people installed in the admirable office which redounds to the benefit of the people. The priest is there for the comfort and enlightenment of souls. He can discharge this function because he himself bears the weight of human frailty. As you look at your Patriarch, look for the priest, the minister of grace, and look for naught else.

"The pastor? A little man, a humble priest, but above all a shepherd. As a young priest, my only aspiration was to become a country priest. . . .

"I will try, quickly and silently, to put myself in touch with all of you, but in a simple and not in a solemn way, and in the manner of the shepherd who counts his sheep one by one."

(*Address upon his arrival in Venice.*)

· *167*

A FATHER AND NOT A POLICEMAN

Upon arriving in Venice in 1953 as Patriarch and Archbishop, he said to a young priest: "I shall conduct myself as a father and not as a policeman."

⁜❖⁜❖⁜

"I want to be good, always, with everybody."

THE DOOR OF THE SHEEP

"We seem to see the first glimmerings of that long-awaited day whose coming Our Lord Jesus Christ invoked with such ardent desire when He said: 'And other sheep I have that are not of this fold. Them also must I bring . . . And there shall be one fold and one shepherd' (John 10:16). Oh, how consoling it would be for our soul to be able to read these words together with those sheep and to meditate on those winning images of the tenth chapter of St. John, especially where Jesus repeats to us: 'I am the door (i.e., the gate through which the sheep enter). If anyone enter by me he shall be safe, and shall go in and out, and shall find pastures' (John 10:9)."

*(Concerning Christian Unity, letter
to the Council Fathers, February 1963.)*

22
THAT THEY MAY BE ONE

❧✳❧✿❧✳❧✿❧✳

✶✶✶✶✶✶✶

WE ARE ALL GUILTY

Of the separated Churches, Pope John said:
"Our duty is to work, even against all hope, for the
union of Christians. We are all guilty, and we Latins,
I mean we Latins in the East, have had and still have
our share of responsibility. If we do not make efforts to
disregard our own convenience and to look far beyond
ourselves, our decline will proceed at the same tempo
as that of the Orientals."

(In the East.)

"We shall not hold an historical trial, We shall not seek to know who was right and who was wrong. The responsibilities are shared. We shall say simply: 'Let us reunite, let us put an end to the dissensions.'"

(*In Rome.*)

✧✱❖✧✱❖✧✱

At the end of an audience with Pope John XXIII, Dr. Fischer, archbishop of Canterbury, made the notable remark:

"The force of his personality is such that he transforms all official contact into a personal experience."

OPEN ARMS

Dr. Arthur Lichtenberger, presiding bishop of the Episcopal Church in the United States, also described his impressions following an audience with Pope John XXIII:

"I felt my heart beat more quickly as I was introduced into the presence of the Sovereign Pontiff, and I felt that apprehension which is natural at the moment of meeting a personage of such high and exalted rank. Moreover I had misgivings about details of protocol. I was preparing to kneel when the Pope, from the far end of his library, came toward me with open arms, so that spontaneously I also opened mine."

NOT JEALOUS

John XXIII officially welcomed the non-Catholic observers on the opening day of the Council. Before addressing himself to them in an intimate allocution in
which he was to say in particular: "Read my heart, you
will find more there than in my words," the Pope's attention was attracted by the dress of the Brothers of
Taizé. The prior and sub-prior of this famous Protestant
religious community had worn their white cowls—their
choir habit. Pope John knew them well but he had never
seen them in this attire during their earlier audiences.
Approaching them, he expressed his surprise.

As the Brothers were making explanations, Pope John
politely interrupted them: "So! You're dressed in white
like me. But you know, I'm not jealous."

That day the observers were very appreciative of the
fact that the Pope sat among them in a chair similar
to the others, one which was only imperceptibly raised
above the rest on a diminutive dais.

I AM JOSEPH, YOUR BROTHER

On October 17, 1960, about two hundred delegates
of the United Jewish Appeal, the great American Jewish welfare organization, were received in audience by
John XXIII in Rome. He welcomed them with open
arms as he quoted a Biblical passage: "I am Joseph, your
brother!"

In a letter to the General of the Franciscan Order,

Pope John—in a reference to the Jews—wrote: "We must employ all means for overcoming the old attitudes, preconceived ideas, and expressions that are none too courteous."

It is well known that John XXIII ordered the deletion of the adjective *perfides* contained in that part of the Good Friday service which is devoted to prayer for the conversion of the Jews.

THE TASK OF THE CHURCH

"In my nightly conversations with the Lord, I always have before me Jesus Crucified, His arms outstretched to receive everyone, because the task of the Catholic and Roman Church is to work for the realization of the prayer of the Divine Master: 'That all may be one.'"

(During the last week of his life.)

23

THE TWO WINGS OF
TRUTH AND GOODNESS

✢✳✤✢✳✤✢✳

✛✳✦✲✛✳✦✲✛✳

MEEK AND HUMBLE OF HEART

"Each pontificate takes its stamp from the pe
who occupies the Chair of Peter. The great teac
of Christ is summarized in these words: 'Learn
Me who am meek and humble of heart.'"

PATIENCE AND CALM

"The strength of the bishop lies in patient, gen
and brotherly goodness."

"Patience and calm, two beautiful qualities."

"The tiny thorns that are endured for the lo
Jesus become roses."

"One must make oneself loved. I must be everyb
bishop."

.

Where charity is lacking, what can we expect?"

Oh, how we must imitate the Lord and be patient men!"

To be always busy and yet never be in the grip of is a foretaste of heaven on earth. There is noth- of interest to me outside the will of God."

Calm of spirit in the face of difficulties constitutes strength."

(*Journal, 1938–1939.*)

THE GOOD SHEPHERD

In the wild forest of news, each wants the world to organized according to his own view. Thus there has talk of a political pope, of a scholarly pope, of a diplomatic pope, when the pope is just the pope. He good shepherd who seeks to reach souls and to upon the truth. Truth and goodness are like two gs. We must not fashion a pope according to our s."

OUR HEART SWELLS
WITH TENDERNESS

Our heart enters your homes, all alight in ardent ctation of the birth of the divine Saviour, and it ls with tenderness as We address to you our greet- and fatherly good wishes. We would like to linger

.

longer at the tables of the poor, in the factories, i
halls of study and of science, at the bedside of
persons and of the aged, in every place where men
and suffer, toiling for themselves and for others,
ing generously with their hands or in the disciplin
the mind and of the heart. Yes, we would like to
our hand on the heads of infants, look into the ey
the young, encourage fathers and mothers to p
their daily task! To all we would like to repeat the v
of the Angel: 'I bring you good news of great joy
a Saviour has been born to you, Who is the Lord.'

(Radio message, Christmas

✦✳✦❀✦✳✦❀✦✳

"Oh, how deeply I feel each morning the signific
of the *Domine non sum dignus* as I hold in my
the sacred Host, that seal of humility and of love

THE TRANQUIL SEA OF GOD'S W

"Let me tell you with the heart of a brother
now more than ever it is a case of closing your eye
hands, of ridding yourself completely of the bagga
your selfhood and of plunging into the sure and
quil sea of God's holy will where alone will you f
measure of peace."

(Letter to a friend,

THE THREE CALLED FRANCIS

y devotions as a boy at home, in the parish church,
side my uncle: Jesus, St. Joseph, and the three
l Francis: Francis of Assisi, Francis Xavier and
is de Sales."

✢✺✛✪✢✺✛✪✢✺

he figure of St. Francis de Sales is not one that can
closed within narrow horizons. It rises before the
, lofty and serene, higher than the mountains of
voy, more serene than the smiling sky reflected in
lue waters of the little lake of Annecy. . . . In
, St. Francis de Sales was the most lovable of all
aints, and God sent him to the world in a very sad
. . . He appeared and he remained as an incar-
n of a strong and smiling piety wherein were fused
rtless poetry of St. Francis of Assisi and the per-
ious love of St. Augustine."

✢✺✛✪✢✺✛✪✢✺

have prayed to St. Andrew to make me taste ever
ore a love for the cross."

✢✺✛✪✢✺✛✪✢✺

verything is made beautiful by the smile of Mary
looks upon our humble actions with a maternal

(Journal, 1938.)

24

OUR SISTER, DEATH

✦✳✿✦✳✦✿✦✳

❀✦❀✦❀✦❀✦❀

I LOVE LIFE

During an audience, Pope John said:

"We will pray for you, for your families. And do
also pray for your Pope. For, to be frank, permit
to tell you that I wish to live a long time. I love life

❀✦❀✦❀✦❀✦❀

"It is good to feel the weight of fatigue. It is
ransom for our sins and is meritorious in obtaining g
in favor of those souls who are the object of our so
tude."

(*Journal, 19*

Not to desire—nor pray for this purpose—to live
er, not even a day longer than the time when the
el of death will come to call for me and take me to
en, as I hope."

(*Spiritual testament, "To the Roncalli family."*)

✦❋✦✤❋✦✤❋✦❋✦

t is an indisputable truth that all of us one day will
ive a visit from our Sister Death, as St. Francis of
si called her. She sometimes presents herself in a
len and unexpected manner. But we shall remain
quil, or better undisturbed, if our tree has known
to yield its fruits. He who has worked well, departs
n the day has ended."

(*At a general audience, March 7, 1961.*)

✦❋✦✤❋✦✤❋✦❋✦

f the Pope can no longer function as the Pope, it is
er that he die."

(*To English bishops during the Council.*)

✦❋✦✤❋✦✤❋✦❋✦

await the arrival of Sister Death calmly and gladly.
all welcome her in a manner that is in keeping with
the circumstances with which it shall please the
d to surround her."

"I feel in my body the beginning of a certain disturbance which must be natural for an old man. I endure it in peace, even if sometimes it is a little painful, and even if I fear its aggravation. It is not pleasant to think about it, but once more I am ready for everything."

(Retreat, November 1961.)

✦✳✦✿✦✳✦✿✦✳

"We run after the Lord who rises up to heaven."

(Ascension Day, 1962.)

ALL DAYS ARE GOOD FOR DYING

"I am untroubled. I have always wanted to do the will of God. Always. Always. I pray for the Church, for the children, for the priests and for the bishops so that they may become saints, and for the whole world."

✦✳✦✿✦✳✦✿✦✳

"All days, like all months, equally belong to the Lord. Thus they are all equally beautiful."

(Journal, 1939.)

✦✳✦✿✦✳✦✿✦✳

"We are entering our eighty-second year. Shall we finish it? All days are good for being born, all days are good for dying."

(Address of December 25, 1962.)

· *185*

"It is good to be crushed by sorrow and by death so that we may rise again."

COURAGE!

John XXIII received the Last Anointing on his death bed. All around him were weeping. Thereupon the Pope, knocking repeatedly on the wooden part of his bed, exclaimed almost angrily:

"Come now! Courage! Courage! It's not yet the Requiem!"

"This bed is an altar. The altar demands a victim. I am ready. I have before me a clear view of my soul, of my priesthood, of the Council, of the Universal Church."

MY BAGS ARE ALWAYS PACKED

Tuesday, May 28, 1963:

"Oh! how grateful I am! To be the object of such tender care and attention moves me and leaves me perfectly in my habitual simplicity, while I feel myself more than ever in communion with all those who suffer in hospitals and in their homes and who are in anguish for different reasons. This interest shown to the Pope, who humbly represents the Lord, must mark a renewal of prayers, of thoughts, and of resolutions for peace, a clear and distinct conviction that what is of value in life is always in the spirit of the Gospel: mildness, goodness, and charity."

"I desire that all receive the mark of my deep gratitude, so that they may draw from it the motive and impulse for mutual brotherly love, and since they wish to remain in union with me. I bless and I encourage . . ."

Friday, May 31, 1963:

"In my vigils at night, I have always kept before me Jesus Crucified with his arms outstretched to receive the whole world. It is the role of the Catholic and Apostolic Church, of the Roman Church, to work for the realization of the prayer of the Divine Master: *Ut unum, ut unum sint.*"

"I am wholly ready to go where the Lord calls me."

"I desire to be dissolved and to be with Christ."

The Pope held his arms in the form of a cross on his bed.

He told Msgr. Rocca: "I thank you for all the services that you have rendered me. We shall continue to love each other in heaven."

Saturday, June 1, 1963:

Pope John asked that the *Magnificat* be recited: "Come, courage! This is not the moment to weep; this is a moment of joy and glory."

"I suffer very much, but with love."

To his secretary: "When it's all over, don't forget to go visit your mother."

The Pope embraced his brothers and said: "I am the resurrection and the life! Jesus! Jesus!"

"Let us pray for papa and mamma. I have always thought about them, and I am happy because in a little while I shall see them again in heaven."

"With death a new life begins, glorification in Christ."

To Cardinal Testa, who seemed to be preparing to leave: "Stay a bit longer!"

To Professor Gasparrini: "Dear Professor, don't be disturbed. My bags are always packed. When the moment to depart arrives, I won't lose any time."

Sunday, June 2, 1963:

"Christ receives me. I am close to Jesus."

"It is a great day for the Church" (it was Pentecost).

Pope John gave a last blessing to the world.

Monday, June 3, 1963:

Pope John XXIII died at 7:45 P.M. after having said: *"Mater mea, fiducia mea"* (My mother, my trust).

At the same moment, Professor Gasparrini, who watched as he drew his last breath, distinctly heard a priest who was celebrating Mass in the adjoining room say:

"Ita missa est."

EPILOGUE

THE HOUSE OF ALL

❧✲❧❀❧✲❧❀❧✲

PEACE

In his encyclical *Pacem in terris,* Pope John XXIII addressed himself, beyond the visible frontiers of the Church, to all men of good will. Thus he recalled to Catholics that the Church belonged to all, believers or not, and that the vocation of all mankind is to be the "people of God."

"Peace I leave with you, my peace I give to you," said Christ on the eve of His death. The Church is therefore under the obligation to proclaim peace to the world, and in particular to work for the peace of arms, an elementary manifestation of charity among men.

Is not the first duty of a pope to be a man of peace? A man of peace in the natural and supernatural sense of this word at one and the same time? What unbeliever, in fact, would take Christianity seriously if religion reserved some indulgence for war?

Now this Pope had been a man of peace in the highest degree. Recalling the last days of his former bishop, Msgr. Radini, whose last invocation was a call for peace, John XXIII wrote in his personal diary:

"I too would like for a prayer for peace to be my last as pope, as the humble Pope John."

"Peace is the house of all."